Stage 1+ Pack A

Floppy's Phonics Fiction

Kate Ruttle

Group/Guided Re

Contents

Cats

Pop!

Mud!

Big, Bad Bug

Hats

A Big Mess

Introduction

Welcome to *Floppy's Phonics*! This series gives you amusing decodable phonic stories featuring all your favourite *Oxford Reading Tree* characters. The books provide the perfect opportunity for consolidation and practice of synthetic phonics within a familiar setting, to build your children's confidence. As well as having a strong phonic focus, each story is a truly satisfying read with lots of opportunities for comprehension, so they are fully in line with the simple view of reading.

Phonic development

The *Floppy's Phonics* stories support a synthetic phonics approach to early reading skills and are fully aligned to *Letters and Sounds*. They should be used for practice and consolidation. The books should be read in the suggested order (see chart on page 3), so that children can benefit from the controlled introduction, revision and consolidation of the phonemes. They can be read before the *Floppy's Phonics Non-fiction* books at the same stage. In addition, they can be used for practice and consolidation after introducing the sounds with other programmes.

The series can be used within Phase 2 of *Letters and Sounds*, to support children as they broaden their knowledge of graphemes and phonemes for use in reading and spelling. The books will help to embed these vital early phonic skills, and help to ensure that children will experience success in reading and thus will be motivated to keep on reading.

Your children will benefit most from reading *Floppy's Phonics* Stage 1+ if they are able to:

- recognize the direction of text on a page
- match words and phrases
- use picture cues and memory to retain characters' names and some tricky high frequency words
- blend and segment CVC words
- recognize the graphemes used in the stories.

Phonic focus

This chart shows which phonemes are introduced and practised in each title.

Title	ORT Stage Book band colour Year group	*Letters and Sounds* phase	Phonemes introduced	Phonemes revisited
Cats	Stage 1+ Pink Reception	Phase Two	s a t p n m o c	
Pop!	Stage 1+ Pink Reception	Phase Two	l d g i	s a t p n m o
Mud!	Stage 1+ Pink Reception	Phase Two	ck u r h	s a t p n m d o g l
Big, Bad Bug	Stage 1+ Pink Reception	Phase Two	b ff	s a t p i n d g o u r h l
Hats	Stage 1+ Pink Reception	Phase Two	e	s a t p i n d g o c u r h b ff
A Big Mess	Stage 1+ Pink Reception	Phase Two	k ff ll ss j	s a t p i n d g o c ck u r h b ff

High frequency and context words

Most of the common words introduced in *Floppy's Phonics* are phonically decodable, using phonic skills and knowledge that are gradually developed through the stories. *Floppy's Phonics* also introduces the high frequency words which are listed in *Letters and Sounds.* High frequency words are common words which occur frequently in children's books. Many of them are decodable, some of them are 'tricky'. The words are defined in line with *Letters and Sounds.*

High frequency (HF) decodable words

Many of the high frequency words are decodable by saying and blending the sounds, and children should practise them regularly so that they can read them automatically as soon as possible.

High frequency (HF) tricky words

Some of the high frequency words are 'tricky', that is, they contain unusual grapheme-phoneme correspondences (e.g. *no, the*). The advice in *Letters and Sounds* is that children should be taught to recognize the phonemes they know within these words and to distinguish these from the tricky bits. For example, in the word *no,* children should be taught to recognize the grapheme *n* and then taught the tricky sound of 'o' in this context.

Context words

In most of the books in *Floppy's Phonics* there are one or two other words, including the characters' names, which cannot be read using phonics alone, but which add to the child's enjoyment and understanding of the story. These words are listed as 'context words'.

The characters in these books are Mum, Dad, Biff, Chip, Kipper, Gran and Floppy. The names of the characters are listed as context words if they are not yet decodable.

The table on page 5 shows the context words, and the Phase 2 high frequency decodable and tricky words which appear in each story.

High frequency and context words used in each book

Cats	HF decodable words	a at not
	HF tricky words	I the
	Context words	Kipper
Pop!	HF decodable words	it in on mum put
	HF tricky words	the
	Context words	Kipper Chip Biff
Mud!	HF decodable words	in on a it got is put
	HF tricky words	the
	Context words	Kipper Chip Biff
Big, Bad Bug	HF decodable words	had a as on in big dad
	HF tricky words	-
	Context words	Kipper Chip
Hats	HF decodable words	a is it on big mum dad
	HF tricky words	the
	Context words	Kipper Chip Gran
A Big Mess	HF decodable words	big had a of in up on it is got mum dad
	HF tricky words	no the
	Context words	Chip Floppy

Comprehension Strategies

Reading is about making meaning, and it is particularly important that a child's earliest reading books offer opportunities for making meaning and telling a complete story. As with all *Oxford Reading Tree* stories, the titles in *Floppy's Phonics* are fun stories which children will really enjoy, and which will give you lots of scope for practising and extending their comprehension skills.

Story	Comprehension strategy taught through these Group/Guided Reading Notes				
	Prediction	Questioning	Clarifying	Summarising	Imagining
Cats	✓	✓	✓		✓
Pop!	✓	✓	✓		✓
Mud!	✓	✓	✓	✓	
Big, Bad Bug	✓		✓		✓
Hats	✓		✓		✓
A Big Mess	✓	✓	✓	✓	✓

Curriculum coverage chart

	Speaking, Listening, Drama	Reading	Writing
Cats			
PNS Literacy Framework (YR)	1.1, 2.1, 2.2 3.1	**W** 5.1, 5.2, 5.4, 5.5, 5.7, 5.9, 5.10 **C** 7.1, 7.2, 8.1, 8.2	11.1
National Curriculum	Working towards level 1		
Scotland (5-14) (P1)	Early level: LIT 0-01A/M/ LIT 0-02A/L/LIT 0-03A/V/LIT 0-04B/C/LIT 0-05D	Early level: LIT 0-01a/ LIT 0-11a/LIT 0-20a/ ENG 0-12a/ LIT 0-13a/ LIT 0-21a/LIT 0-14a/LIT 0-07a/LIT 0-16a/ ENG 0-17a	Early level: LIT 0-01a/ LIT 0-11a/LIT 0-20a/ ENG 0-12a/LIT 0-13a/LIT 0-21a/LIT 0-21b/LIT 0-26a
N. Ireland (P1)	Attention and Listening: 1, 4, 5 Phonological Awareness: 5, 2 Social use of language: 3, 4, 6 Language and thinking: 1, 4, 6, 7, 5, 11 Extended Vocabulary: 2 Progression: 1, 2, 3, 5, 7	Reading: 1, 2, 4, 5, 6, 7, 8, 11, 12 Progression: 1, 4, 5,	Writing: 1, 3, 4, 6 Progression: 1, 4, 2, 3,
Wales (Foundation Stage)	Skills: 1, 2, 6, 7, 8, 3, 9, 12, 13 Range: 1, 4, 2, 5, 6	Skills: 1, 2, 3, 4, 5, 8 Range: 1, 2, 3, 5, 6	Skills: 1, 2, 3, 4, 6, 8, Range: 1, 2, 3, 4,
Pop!			
PNS Literacy Framework (YR)	1.1, 2.1, 2.2 4.1	**W** 5.1, 5.2, 5.4, 5.5, 5.9, 5.10 **C** 7.1, 7.2, 8.1, 8.2, 8.3	9.1
National Curriculum	Working towards level 1		

Curriculum coverage chart

	Speaking, Listening, Drama	Reading	Writing
Scotland (5-14) (P1)	Early level: LIT 0-01A/M/ LIT 0-02A/L/LIT 0-03A/V/LIT 0-04B/C/LIT 0-05D	Early level: LIT 0-01a/ LIT 0-11a/LIT 0-20a/ ENG 0-12a/ LIT 0-13a/ LIT 0-21a/LIT 0-14a/LIT 0-07a/LIT 0-16a/ENG 0-17a	Early level: LIT 0-01a/ LIT 0-11a/LIT 0-20a/ ENG 0-12a/LIT 0-13a/LIT 0-21a/LIT 0-21b/LIT 0-26a
N. Ireland (P1)	Attention and Listening: 1, 2, 4, 5 Phonological Awareness: 5, 4 Social use of language: 1, 2, 3, 4, 6 Language and thinking: 1, 2, 3, 4, 5, 6, 7, Extended Vocabulary: 1, 2, 3 Progression: 1, 2, 3, 4, 5, 7	Reading: 1, 2, 4, 5, 6, 7, 8, 11, 12 Progression: 1, 4, 5,	Writing: 1, 3, 4, 6 Progression: 1, 4, 2, 3, 5
Wales Key Stage 1	Skills: 1, 2, 3, 6, 7, 8, 9, 10, 12 Range: 1, 2, 3, 4, 5, 6, 7	Skills: 1, 2, 3, 4, 5, 8 Range: 1, 2, 3, 5, 6	Skills: 1, 2, 3, 4, 6, 8, Range: 1, 2, 3, 4, 5
Mud!			
PNS Literacy Framework (YR)	1.1, 2.1, 2.2	**W** 5.1, 5.2, 5.4, 5.5, 5.9, 5.10 **C** 7.1, 7.2, 8.1, 8.2, 8.3	9.1
National Curriculum	Working towards level 1		
Scotland (5-14) (P1)	Early level: LIT 0-01A/M/ LIT 0-02A/L/LIT 0-03A/V/ LIT 0-04B/C/LIT 0-05D	Early level: LIT 0-01a/LIT 0-11a/LIT 0-20a/ENG 0-12a/LIT 0-13a/LIT 0-21a/ LIT 0-14a/LIT 0-07a/LIT 0-16a/ENG 0-17a	Early level: LIT 0-01a/ LIT 0-11a/LIT 0-20a/ENG 0-12a/LIT 0-13a/LIT 0-21a/ LIT 0-21b/LIT 0-26a
N. Ireland (P1)	Attention and Listening: 1, 2, 4, 5 Phonological Awareness: 5, Social use of language: 2, 3, 4, 6 Language and thinking: 1, 2, 4, 5, 6, 7, 8, 9, 10, 11 Extended Vocabulary: 2 Progression: 1, 2, 3, 5, 7	Reading: 1, 2, 3, 4, 5, 6, 7, 8, 11, 12 Progression: 1, 4, 5,	Writing: 1,2, 3, 4, 5, 7 Progression: 1, 2, 3, 4,
Wales Key Stage 1	Skills: 1, 2, 3, 6, 7, 8, 12 Range: 1, 4, 5, 6, 7	Skills: 1, 2, 3, 4, 5, 8 Range: 1, 2, 3, 5, 6	Skills: 1, 2, 3, 4, 6, 8, 9, 10 Range: 1, 2, 3, 4,

Curriculum coverage chart

	Speaking, Listening, Drama	Reading	Writing
A Big, Bad Bug			
PNS Literacy Framework (YR)	1.1, 1.5 2.1, 2.2 3.2	(W) 5.1, 5.2, 5.4, 5.5, 5.8, 5.9, 5.10 (C) 7.1, 7.2, 8.1, 8.2, 8.3	11.1
National Curriculum	Working towards level 1		
Scotland (5-14) (P1)	Early level: LIT 0-01A/M/LIT 0-02A/L/LIT 0-03A/V/LIT 0-04B/C/LIT 0-05D	Early level: LIT 0-01a/LIT 0-11a/LIT 0-20a/ENG 0-12a/LIT 0-13a/LIT 0-21a/LIT 0-14a/LIT 0-07a/LIT 0-16a/ENG 0-17a	Early level: LIT 0-01a/LIT 0-11a/LIT 0-20a/ENG 0-12a/LIT 0-13a/LIT 0-21a/LIT 0-21b/LIT 0-26a
N. Ireland (P1)	Attention and Listening: 1, 4, 5 Phonological Awareness: 2, 4, 5, Social use of language: 3, 4, 5 Language and thinking: 1, 4, 6, 7, Extended Vocabulary: 2, 3 Progression: 1, 2, 3, 5, 6, 7	Reading: 1, 2, 3, 4, 5, 6, 7, 8, 11, 12 Progression: 1, 4, 5, 7, 9	Writing: 1, 3, 4, 6, 7 Progression: 1, 2, 3, 4, 5
Wales Key Stage 1	Skills: 1, 2, 3, 6, 7, 8, 10 Range: 1, 2, 3, 4, 7	Skills: 1, 2, 3, 4, 5, 7, 8 Range: 1, 2, 3, 5, 6	Skills: 1, 2, 3, 4, 5, 6, 8, 9, Range: 1, 2, 3, 4,
Hats			
PNS Literacy Framework (YR)	1.1, 1.5 2.1, 2.2	(W) 5.1, 5.2, 5.4, 5.5, 5.9, 5.10 (C) 7.1, 7.2, 8.1, 8.2	9.1
National Curriculum	Working towards level 1		
Scotland (5-14) (P1)	Early level: LIT 0-01A/M/LIT 0-02A/L/LIT 0-03A/V/LIT 0-04B/C/LIT 0-05D	Early level: LIT 0-01a/LIT 0-11a/LIT 0-20a/ENG 0-12a/LIT 0-13a/LIT 0-21a/LIT 0-14a/LIT 0-07a/LIT 0-16a/ENG 0-17a	Early level: LIT 0-01a/LIT 0-11a/LIT 0-20a/ENG 0-12a/LIT 0-13a/LIT 0-21a/LIT 0-21b/LIT 0-26a

Curriculum coverage chart

	Speaking, Listening, Drama	Reading	Writing
N. Ireland (P1)	Attention and Listening: 1, 2, 4, 5 Phonological Awareness: 4, 5, Social use of language: 3, 4, Language and thinking: 1, 4, 6, 7, 8, 9, 10, 11 Extended Vocabulary: 1, 2, 3 Progression: 1, 2, 3, 5, 6, 7, 9	Reading: 1, 2, 4, 5, 6, 7, 8, 11, 12 Progression: 1, 4, 5,	Writing: 1, 3, 4, 6, 7 Progression: 1, 4,
Wales Key Stage 1	Skills: 1, 2, 3, 6, 7, 8, Range: 1, 2, 3, 4, 5, 7	Skills: 1, 2, 3, 4, 5, 8 Range: 1, 2, 3, 5, 6	Skills: 1, 2, 3, 4, 6, 8, 10 Range: 1, 2, 3, 4, 5
A Big Mess			
PNS Literacy Framework (YR)	1.1, 2.1, 2.2	**W** 5.1, 5.2, 5.4, 5.5, 5.6, 5.9, 5.10 **C** 7.1, 7.2, 8.1, 8.2	6.1 10.1
National Curriculum	Working towards level 1		
Scotland (5-14) (P1)	Early level: LIT 0-01A/M/ LIT 0-02A/L/LIT 0-03A/V/LIT 0-04B/C/LIT 0-05D	Early level: LIT 0-01a/ LIT 0-11a/LIT 0-20a/ ENG 0-12a/LIT 0-13a/ LIT 0-21a/LIT 0-14a/ LIT 0-07a/LIT 0-16a/ENG 0-17a	Early level: LIT 0-01a/ LIT 0-11a/LIT 0-20a/ ENG 0-12a/LIT 0-13a/ LIT 0-21a/LIT 0-21b/LIT 0-26a
N. Ireland (P1)	Attention and Listening: 1, 2, 4, 5 Phonological Awareness: 4, 5, Social use of language: 3, 4, Language and thinking: 1, 4, 5, 6, 7, 8, 9, 10, 11 Extended Vocabulary: 1, 2, 3 Progression: 1, 2, 3, 4, 5, 6, 7, 8, 9	Reading: 1, 2, 3, 4, 5, 6, 7, 8, 11, 12 Progression: 1, 4, 5,	Writing: 1, 2, 3, 4, 5, 6, 7 Progression: 1, 2, 3, 4, 5, 6, 7
Wales Key Stage 1	Skills: 1, 2, 3, 6, 7, 8, 9, 10, 11 Range: 1, 4, 6, 7	Skills: 1, 2, 3, 4, 5, 7, 8 Range: 1, 2, 3, 4, 5, 6	Skills: 1, 2, 3, 4, 6, 8, 10, 12 Range: 1, 2, 3, 4, 5

Cats

> **C** = Language comprehension   **AF** = QCA Assessment focus
>
> **W** = Word recognition

Guided or group reading

Phonic Focus:

Phonemes introduced in this book: s, a, t, p, n, m, o, c

Introducing the book

C *(Predicting)* Read the title, pointing to the word, and showing the picture. Encourage children to use prediction: *What do you think this book is going to be about?*

● Look through the book, talking about what happens on each page. Discuss why Kipper and his friends might dress up as cats. Use some of the high frequency words as you discuss the story (see chart on page 5).

Strategy check

Remind the children to read from left to right and to sound out words when they can.

Independent reading

● Ask children to read the story aloud. Praise and encourage them while they read, and prompt as necessary.

C *(Clarifying)* Ask children to explain what the book is about.

Assessment Check that the children:

● *(AF1)* use phonic knowledge to sound out and blend the phonemes in words (see chart on page 5).

● *(AF2)* use comprehension skills to work out what is happening. Are they clear why Kipper and his friends are dressing up?

● *(AF1)* Make a note of any difficulties the children encounter and of strategies they use to solve problems.

Returning to the text

C *(Questioning, Clarifying)* Ask children *What are the children in the book doing?*

C *(Clarifying)* Ask children to explain how Kipper becomes 'the top cat'.

Assessment *(AF1)* Discuss any words the children found tricky and talk about strategies used.

Group and independent reading activities

Objective Read some high frequency words (5.7).

W Page 1: Ask the children to point as you read the words *I am*. Can they point to each of the words separately?

● Can they find each of the words elsewhere on the page (e.g. in the speech bubble)?

● How many times can they find each word in the book?

● Can they see the words elsewhere in the classroom, e.g. on wall displays, notices, environmental print?

Assessment *(AF1)* Can the children identify each of the words when you point to them on different pages in the book?

Objective Link sounds and letters, naming and sounding letters (5.2).

W On a whiteboard, write the name *Pat*. Ask the children to say the sounds, then read the name. Repeat for *Mat.* Look at the two names. What is different? What is the same? Do the words rhyme?

● Ask the children to look through the book, copying names. Discuss how they might recognize names.

● Can they find another pair of names that rhyme? (*Pam, Sam, Tam*)

Assessment *(AF1)* Can the children say the sounds then read the words of the CVC names (e.g. *Tom, Tam*)?

Objective Hear and say sounds in words in the order in which they occur (5.4).

(W) **You will need:** Plastic/ wooden alphabet letters: s, a, t, p, n, m, o, c.

- Ask the children to sound-talk the word *o-n*. How many sounds/ phonemes are there?

- Can one of the children find the letters they need to make *on*? Ask them to listen carefully, say the sounds, then decide which order they need to go in. Explore other VC words, asking the children to sound-talk and then make the words (e.g. *as, at, an, am, on*).

Assessment *(AF1)* Can the children hear and represent the sounds in these words?

Objective Show an understanding of the story elements, e.g. main character, sequence, openings (8. 2).

(C) *(Clarifying)* Can the children explain what they think is happening in the book? Ask questions like *Which creature are the children dressed up as? Can you find a different creature? What does Kipper say to the dog? Why?*

(C) *(Predicting) What do you think the story in Kipper's play is about? Can you tell me what happens in the story?*

Assessment *(AF3)* Can children clearly explain what the context for the book is?

Speaking, listening and drama activities

Objective Interact with others, negotiating plans and activities (3. 1).

Let the children plan their own version of the play in the book. Ask them to decide who will be a cat, who will be a dog and who will be the top cat – or will they all hiss at the dog?

Assessment Observe the children's discussion. Note who is able to negotiate, who takes a lead role, who is uncooperative.

Writing activities

Objective Writes their own name and other things such as labels and captions (11.1).

You will need: The words *I* and *am* in a word bank. Some children may benefit from a name card.

- Ask the children to draw themselves as one of the cats from the book.
- Under their pictures, ask them to write *I am [name].*

Assessment *(Writing AF8)* Are children able to write their names without support? How accurately can they copy?

Pop!

> **C** = Language comprehension   **AF** = QCA Assessment focus
>
> **W** = Word recognition

Guided or group reading

Phonic Focus:

Phonemes introduced in this book: i, d, g, l, Phonemes revisited in this book: s, a, t, p, n, m, o

Introducing the book

C *(Predicting)* Read the title, pointing to the word, and showing the picture. Encourage the children to use prediction: *What do you think this book is going to be about?*

● Look through the book, talking about what happens on each page. Discuss why the book is called *Pop!*. Use the high frequency words as you discuss the story (see chart on page 5).

Strategy check

Remind the children to read from left to right and to sound out words when they can.

Independent reading

● Ask the children to read the story aloud. Praise and encourage them while they read, and prompt as necessary.

C *(Clarifying)* Ask the children to explain what the book is about.

Assessment Check that the children:

● *(AF1)* use phonic knowledge to sound out and blend the phonemes in words (see chart on page 5).

● *(AF2)* use comprehension skills to work out what is happening. *What are Mum and the children doing in the book?*

● *(AF1)* Make a note of any difficulties the children encounter and of strategies they use to solve problems.

Returning to the text

C *(Questioning, Clarifying)* Ask the children *What are the children in the book doing?*

Assessment *(AF1)* Discuss any words the children found tricky and talk about strategies used.

Group and independent reading activities

Objective Link sounds and letters, naming and sounding letters (5.2).

W Write the words *pop* and *pot* on a whiteboard. Ask the children to say the sounds in each word, then to tell you the whole word. *Are the words the same? What is the same? What is different?*

● Write li and lid. *'What's the same? What is different?* Write *tp* and *top*. *What is the same? What is different?'* Repeat for other words.

Assessment *(AF1)* Write the letters *op.* Can the children tell what else you need to make *pop?*

Objective Explore and experiment with sounds words and letters (5. 1).

W **You will need:** Plastic/ wooden letters: s, a, t, p, i, n, m, d, g, o, l

● Use the letters to make the word *pop.* Give one of the children the *t.* Ask them to use it instead of the first *p.* Can the children read the new word?

● Make *pop* again. This time replace the final *p* with the *t.* What is the word this time?

● Starting with *pot*, ask one of the children to replace the *o* with an *a.* Now which word have you made?

● Continue to ask the children to swap one letter at a time to make a new word. Each time, they should say the letters and then read the new word.

Assessment *(AF1)* Can the children read words composed of the target letters?

Objective Retell narratives in the correct sequence, drawing on the language patterns of stories (8.3).

(C) *(Clarifying)* Give each of the children a sticker showing the name of one of the characters in the book.

- Ask the children to put themselves in the right order according to the order in which people helped to make the popcorn. (*Kipper, Biff, Mum, Chip*)
- Ask each child to find out what they did.
- One at a time, ask the children to read their page aloud, each child talking about their character's contribution.

Assessment *(AF2)* Can each child say their sentence in the correct sequence?

Speaking, listening and drama activities

Objective Use language to imagine and recreate roles and experiences (4.1).

(C) *(Oral language development)* Use objects from your domestic play corner and kitchen to recreate the cooking experience.

- Can the children follow the sequence of events in the book to 'make' their own popcorn? Encourage talk around what is going on.
- Leave the children to play with the kitchen equipment. Observe how they extend the roles from the book.

Assessment Observe the children's play. Note who is able to develop and extend roles, based on the information and ideas in the book.

Writing activities

Objective   Attempts writing for various purposes (9.1).

You will need: Zig-zag books, coloured pens, pencils.

Ask the children to illustrate their own book about making popcorn stage by stage. Allow them to use *Pop!* as a reminder if they wish. Ask them to write sentences or captions for their pictures.

Assessment   Check that children's mark making is meaningful. Are the children able to correctly represent some of the sounds in the words?

Mud!

> **C** = Language comprehension   **AF** = QCA Assessment focus
>
> **W** = Word recognition

Guided or group reading

Phonic Focus:
Phase 2 phonemes introduced in this book: u, r, h, ck
Phase 2 phonemes revisited: s, a, t, p, i, n, m, d, g, o, l

Introducing the book

C *(Predicting)* Read the title, pointing to the word, and showing the picture. Encourage children to use prediction: *What do you think is going to happen in this story?*

● Look through the book, talking about what happens on each page. Were the children's predictions correct? Use some of the high frequency words as you discuss the story (see chart on page 5).

Strategy check
Remind the children to read from left to right and to sound out words.

Independent reading

● Ask the children to read the story aloud. Praise and encourage them while they read, and prompt as necessary.

C *(Clarifying)* Ask the children to explain why Kipper is in the bath at the end of the book.

Assessment Check that the children:

● *(AF1)* use phonic knowledge to sound out and blend the phonemes in words (see chart on page 5).

● *(AF2)* use comprehension skills to work out what is happening.

● *(AF1)* Make a note of any difficulties the children encounter and of strategies they use to solve problems.

Returning to the text

C *(Clarifying)* Ask the children *What happened in the story?*

C *(Clarifying)* Ask the children to explain why Kipper had to wear a rug.

Assessment *(AF1)* Discuss any words the children found tricky and talk about the strategies used.

Group and independent reading activities

Objective Explore and experiment with sounds, words and letters (5.1).

W Ask the children to find all the words containing *o* on page 1. (*on, got, log, bog*) Write the words.

● Can the children tell you which of the words rhyme? How can they tell?

● Can they think of any other words that rhyme with *log* and *bog*? (e.g. *dog, fog, mog*) Can they show you how to spell the words?

● Explore words that can be made by changing the vowel in the word *bog.* Can children read and write the words *bag, big, bug*?

Assessment *(AF1)* Can children identify the pairs of words that rhyme and suggest more rhyming words?

Objective Hear and say sounds in words in the order in which they occur (5.5).

W **You will need:** Plastic/ wooden letters: o, n, a, l, g, t, p, s, m, i, d, b, h, u, r.

● Use the letters to make the word *bog.* Ask one of the children to swap the *b* for a *d.* Can the children read the new word?

● Now replace the *o* with an *i* to make *dig;* then the *g* with a *p* to make *dip.* Continue to ask the children to swap one letter at a time to make a new word. Each time, they should say the letters and then read the new word.

Assessment *(AF1)* Can the children read words composed of the target letters?

Objective Show an understanding of story elements such as sequence of events (8.3).

C *(Summarizing)* Ask the children to identify what Kipper is doing on each page.

- Agree a sequence of events which sequences Kipper's day.

- Using the words *before* and *after* ask the children questions about the events, e.g. *What happened* after *Kipper got on the log*? *What happened* before *Kipper put on the rug?*

- Encourage the children to look at the book when they answer the questions.

Assessment *(AF2)* Can the children answer questions involving *before* and *after*?

Speaking, listening and drama activities

Objective Sustain attentive listening, responding to what they have heard with comments, questions or actions (2.2).

- **C** *(Questioning)* Give different children labels to wear showing the names of the different family members.

- Each child should take it in turn to answer questions, in role.

- Support the other children with asking questions. Introduce the children to the question words *what, where, when, why* and *how*.

Assessment *(AF3)* Observe the children's talk. Note who is able to frame and to answer questions in role.

Writing activities

Objective Attempts writing for various purposes (9.1).

You will need: Some children may benefit from a word bank and an alphabet chart.

- Ask the children to find the speech bubbles *Kipper is in the mud*! (page 5), *Mud on the dog* (page 7) and *Mud in the tub* (page 8).

- Let the children draw somewhere or something else with mud on it or in it. Can they write a label for their picture?

- Children could use ICT to communicate their ideas.

Assessment Can the children use known letters to represents sounds in the words they need?

Big, Bad Bug

> **C** = Language comprehension **AF** = QCA Assessment focus
>
> **W** = Word recognition

Guided or group reading

Phonic Focus:

Phase 2 phonemes introduced in this book: b, ff

Phase 2 phonemes revisited in this book: s, a, t, p, i, n, d, g, o, c, u, r, h, b, l

Introducing the book

C *(Predicting)* Read the title, pointing to the words, and showing the picture. Encourage children to use prediction: *What do you think is going to happen in this story?*

● Look through the book, talking about what happens on each page. Can children identify any of the bugs?

Strategy check

Remind the children to read from left to right and to sound out words.

Independent reading

● Ask the children to read the story aloud. Praise and encourage them while they read, and prompt as necessary.

C *(Clarifying)* Ask the children to explain what the story is about. *Did Dad find a bug?*

Assessment Check that the children:

● *(AF1)* use phonic knowledge to sound out and blend the phonemes in words (see chart on page 5).

● *(AF2)* use comprehension skills to work out what is happening.

● *(AF1)* Make a note of any difficulties the children encounter and of strategies they use to solve problems.

Returning to the text

(C) *(Clarifying)* Look at page 4. Can the children tell you where Chip found his bug?

(W) Look at page 4. Ask them to sound out the word *c-u-p cup*.

(C) *(Clarifying)* Ask *Where did Dad's bug come from?*

Assessment *(AF1)* Discuss any words the children found tricky and talk about strategies used.

Group and independent reading activities

Objective Hear and say sounds in words in the order in which they occur (5.4).

(W) Give each child three counters. Tell them that they will need to use one counter to show each of the sounds they hear in a word.

● Model the task. Say the word *big.* Repeat it, this time allowing a slight pause between each of the sounds *b-i-g.* Say the word one more time with distinct pauses between each sound *b – i – g.* As you say each sound, push one counter forward, so the children see you have all three counters pushed forwards.

● Now work together to consider the word *bug.* Go through the processes as before with the children.

● Can the children work independently to do the same task for the words: *bad, pot, bag, cup, in, on?*

Assessment *(AF1)* Can children show how many sounds there are – and tell you which sounds they are – for some of the words on page 5?

Objective Use phonic knowledge to write simple, regular words (5.8).

(W) Write the words: *A bug on a* and tell the children that you are going to tell them different ways to finish the sentence and ask them to spell the final word each time.

● Start with *cup.* Before children write, sound-talk the word together *c-u-p cup.* Can children show you on their fingers how many sounds there are in the word and the order in which they have to represent them? Ask children to write the word *cup.*

- Repeat for other places the children found or kept bugs: *lid, bud, log, bag, pot.*

Assessment *(AF1)* Look at the letters each child used to represent each of the words. Are they showing 3 letters each time? Are they the appropriate choice of letters?

Objective Extend vocabulary, exploring the meanings and sounds of new words (1.5).

C *(Imagining)* Reread the story aloud to the children.

Look at the way Dad describes his big, bad bug. It's *as big as a rat.*

- Show children a potato. What else might a potato bug be as big as?
- Explore ideas and language. Help the children to develop lots of ideas for completing the simile, e.g. *As big as a: bat, can, apple, camera, ball, computer mouse.*

Assessment Can each child suggest an appropriate way to complete the simile?

Speaking, listening and drama activities

Objective Use talk to organise, sequence and clarify thinking (3.2).

You will need: potatoes or small boxes, pipe cleaners, matchsticks, straws, wobbly eyes, tissue paper, coloured cellophane ... and any other appropriate craft pieces.

C *(Oral language development)* Give the children the opportunity to make their own version of Dad's big, bad bug.

- Reread the book together, focusing on Dad. At which point did he decide to make his own bug?
- Let the children work in pairs, as independently as possible, working together to build their own big, bad bug.

Assessment Listen to the children's use of language for negotiating, organizing, sequencing and clarifying their thoughts.

Writing activities

Objective Writes things such as labels (11.1).

- Ask the children to draw all of the places the children found bugs in the book.
- They can then label their drawings, sounding out the letters they need for each word. They could use computers for this activity.

Assessment Check which sounds children are able to represent in each word.

Hats

> **C** = Language comprehension   **AF** = QCA Assessment focus
>
> **W** = Word recognition

Guided or group reading

Phonic Focus:

Phase 2 phoneme introduced: e

Phase 2 phonemes revisited: s, a, t, p, i, n, d, g, o, c, u, r, h, b, ff

Introducing the book

W Can children read the title? Talk about the use of the final –s. Do children know what it is used for?

C *(Predicting)* Encourage children to use prediction: *Where might the family be going? Why might they all be wearing these hats?*

● Look through the book, talking about what happens on each page. Use some of the high frequency words as you discuss the story (see chart on page 5).

Strategy check

Remind the children to read from left to right and to sound out words.

Independent reading

● Ask the children to read the story aloud. Praise and encourage them while they read, and prompt as necessary.

C *(Clarifying)* Ask the children to explain which hat they liked best, and why.

Assessment Check that children:

● *(AF1)* use phonic knowledge to sound out and blend the phonemes in words (see chart on page 5).

● *(AF2)* use comprehension skills to work out what is happening.

● *(AF1)* Make a note of any difficulties the children encounter and of strategies they use to solve problems.

Returning to the text

(W) What does Gran have on her hat? Talk about strategies for reading *pom-pom*.

Assessment *(AF1)* Discuss any words the children found tricky and talk about strategies used.

Group and independent reading activities

Objective Explore and Experiment with sounds (5.1).

(W) **You will need**: little whiteboards and pens.

● Ask the children to sound-talk, then write the word *h-a-t hat*.

● Can they rub out the 'h' and write another letter to make a new word (e.g. *bat, cat, fat, mat, sat*)?

● What can children tell you about the two words, *hat* and their new word? Are there any other rhyming words they can write?

● Repeat the process with other words from the book e.g. (*tap, top, big, mad*).

Assessment *(AF1)* Can the children all write their initial word and then think of and write a rhyming word each time?

Objective Read some high frequency words (5.9).

(W) Reread the text on pages 2 and 3 and talk about the hats.

● Can the children find the word *has* on the page? Can they sound-talk the word? What do they notice about the final sound? Which letter do they usually associate with that sound (z)?

● Can they identify another word on pages 2 and 3 which has the same final sound? (*is*)

● Talk about the fact that sometimes, letters may be pronounced differently at different places in the word.

● Show children the word *hiss*. Can they read the word? Talk about the final sound. *How many letters are used to show it?*

● Can children find another word on page 4 where more than one letter is used to show the last sound in a word? (*Biff*)

Assessment *(AF1)* Can children read the words *miss, toss, fuss*?

Objective To hear and say sounds in words in the order in which they occur (5.4).

W **You will need** four counters for each child; a whiteboard to write on.

- Say the word *hat.* Can the children repeat the whole word, then segment it into its sounds (*h-a-t*)? Ask the children to push one counter forwards for each sound as they say it.

- Repeat for the word *hats.* How many sounds? (4)

- Do the same for the words *top, tap, sun, big, mad, red.* Where appropriate, also include the plural: *taps, suns.*

- Revisit all of the words you have used, but this time, you say the sounds (e.g. *h-a-t*) and ask the children to blend the sounds and say the word.

Assessment *(AF1)* Can the children blend and segment all the words?

Speaking, listening and drama activities

Objective Extend vocabulary exploring the meanings and sounds of new words (1.5).

You will need: hats. You can have real hats, small-world hats or pictures from catalogues.

C *(Imagining)*

- Select a hat and show it to the children. Make a list of words to describe the hat. They can describe colour, texture, pattern, type of hat or any features of the hat. Scribe the words the children suggest, congratulating them on interesting and exciting words.

- Suggest who might wear each of the hats. Are they most likely to be men or women? Adults or children? Is there an occasion or type of weather that might be most appropriate for the type of hat?

- Ask children to put a hat on, or pretend to put it on, and to mime what the person wearing the hat might do.

- Take photographs of the children as they work.

Assessment Can the children suggest descriptive words to talk about each of the hats?

Writing activities

Objective Attempts writing for various purposes (9.1).

- Use the photographs or pictures of hats from the previous activity.
- Ask the children to select an image and to write a list of words to describe the hat or its wearer.

Assessment *(AF1)* Can children write CVC words unaided? Can they use their phonic knowledge to make plausible attempts at more complex words?

A Big Mess

> **C** = Language comprehension   **AF** = QCA Assessment focus
>
> **W** = Word recognition

Guided or group reading

Phonic Focus:

Phase 2 phonemes introduced in this book: k, ll, ss

Phase 3 phonemes introduced in this book: j

Phase 2 phonemes revisited: s, a, t, p, i, n, m, d, g, o, e, u, r, h, b, f

Introducing the book

W Encourage the children to sound out the title.

C *(Predicting)* Encourage the children to use prediction: *What do you think is going to happen in this story?*

● Look through the book, talking about what is happening on each page. Use some of the high frequency words as you discuss the story (see chart on page 5).

Strategy check

Remind the children to read from left to right and to sound out words.

Independent reading

● Ask the children to read the story aloud. Praise and encourage them while they read, and prompt as necessary.

C *(Summarizing)* Ask the children to retell the story in just two or three sentences.

Assessment Check that the children:

● *(AF1)* use phonic knowledge to sound out and blend the phonemes in words (see chart on page 5).

● *(AF2)* use comprehension skills to work out what is happening.

● *(AF1)* Make a note of any difficulties the children encounter and of strategies they use to solve problems.

Returning to the text

(C) *(Questioning, Clarifying)* Ask the children *Why did Dad spill the jam?*

Assessment *(AF1)* Discuss any words the children found tricky and talk about strategies used.

Group and independent reading activities

Objective Read simple words by sounding out and blending from left to right (5.6).

(W) Pages 2 and 3: can the children find two words on these pages that rhyme? (*pan/ran*). *What is different? What is the same?*

● Can they suggest more words that rhyme with *pan*? (e.g. *can, fan, man, tan*)

Assessment *(AF1)* Ask each child to read a CVC word from the book by blending the phonemes. The child should say each of the individual phonemes aloud, then blend them to make the word.

Objective To use phonic knowledge to read simple regular words (5.10).

(W) You will need: four counters for each child; a whiteboard to write on.

● Say the word *mess*. Ask the children to push forward one counter to represent each sound in the word. How many counters do they need? (3: *m-e-ss*).

● Write the word *mess* on the whiteboard. Count the number of letters. Does it match the number of sounds?

● Which sound is shown by more than one letter?

● Repeat for words like *less, fell, well, tell, bell.*

Assessment *(AF1)* Can the children read the words they have made?

Objective Show understanding of story elements, e.g. main character, sequence, openings (8.2).

(C) *(Summarizing)* Show an understanding of elements in stories such as characters and sequence of events.

● Reread the book to the children.

- Model taking on the role of Dad. In role, explain what happened in the story. Explain what happened, whose fault the mess was and why.

- Ask one of the children to take on the role of Dad and to explain what happened. What information can they add?

- Encourage other children to take on the role of Mum, Biff or Chip, or of the man with the kit. How might views of what happened vary?

Assessment (AF3) Make observations about children's participation in the activity and their engagement with the events in the story.

Speaking, listening and drama activities

Objective Show understanding of story elements, e.g. main character, sequence, openings (8.2).

C (*Imagining*) Use language to imagine and recreate roles and experiences (4.1).

- Reread the book to the children. Discuss other ways in which Floppy can help the family to make a mess.

- Let the children role play different scenarios. The only constant is that in each scenario, Floppy has to be the cause of making a mess. Encourage the children to draw on their wider knowledge of reading, particularly of Oxford Reading Tree stories.

- Take photographs of the children in their role play.

Assessment (AF3) Can the children imagine and role play different scenarios? Observe those who lead with suggestions and those who follow or are uninterested.

Writing activities

Objective Attempt writing for various purposes (10.1).

C (*Sequencing*) **You will need:** photographs from the activity above.

- Remind the children of the role plays they did where Floppy caused a mess.

- Ask the children to draw a sequence of three pictures: in the first a member of the family has to be doing something; in the second Floppy has to interrupt the activity and cause a mess; the third picture should show the consequence of the mess.
- Ask the children to attempt to write captions to explain what is happening in each of the pictures. They could use computers for this activity.

Assessment *(AF1)* Can the children sequence the activities? Can they use enough sounds in their writing so that it can be read?